Banana Monster

Peter Bently

QEB Publishing

Charlie was telling his baby brother Chester a story about monsters.

"Monsters are huge and scary!"

said Charlie.

"Oo-ooh!"
said Chester.
"I hope I never
meet one!"

"Now, I'm a little hungry. Time to visit my secret stash of bananas!"

Charlie crept through the bushes. Then he stopped.

"Uh-oh. What was that noise?"

He could hear someone eating his bananas!

"Eek!"

cried Charlie.
"It must be... a
monster!"

Charlie ran back
home to his mom.

"What's the matter?" asked Mom.

"I think there's a **monster** in the bushes!" said Charlie.

Suddenly they heard a loud grunting sound.

"It's the monster!" shivered Charlie. "Asleep in the bushes!"

"Why don't you climb that tree and look?" said Mom. "You'll be safe up there."

Quietly as a mouse,
Charlie started to climb.

Carefully...

does...

it.

Just a little closer...

At last Charlie
looked down into
the bushes and saw...

the monster!

It was Chester—asleep
after eating all Charlie's
bananas!

Notes for parents and teachers

• Before reading the book with a child, or children, look at the cover and see if they can guess what the story is about.

• Read the story, then ask the child(ren) to read it to you. Help them with unfamiliar words and praise their efforts. Can they guess what happens at the end? Which pictures do they like best?

• In the story, Charlie tells his baby brother Chester a scary story about monsters. Ask the children to explain, in their own words, how Chester ends up scaring Charlie.

• Have the children ever seen a real chimpanzee? Chimps are our closest relatives in the animal world. How are they similar to humans, and how are they different? Discuss where chimps live and what they like to eat.

• Turn the story of Charlie and Chester into a play. One child can be Charlie and two others can play Chester and Mom. The rest of the children can be other chimps or different jungle animals—or the monsters that Charlie imagines.

Design and Illustration: Fiona Hajée

Copyright © QEB Publishing, Inc. 2011

Published in the United States by
QEB Publishing
3 Wrigley, Suite A
Irvine, CA 92618

www.qed-publishing.co.uk

A CIP record for this book is available from the Library of Congress.

ISBN 978 1 60992 072 2

Printed in China

Picture credits (t=top, b=bottom, l=left, r=right, c=center)
FLPA front cover Cyril Ruoso/Minden Pictures, 1 Jurgen & Christine Sohns, 2 Fritz Polking, 3 Cyril Ruoso/Minden Pictures, 4 & 5 Jurgen & Christine Sohns, 8 Suzi Eszterhas/Minden Pictures, 10 Gerard Lacz, 12–13 & 14–15 Jurgen & Christine Sohns, 16–17 Terry Whittaker, 18l and 18r Cyril Ruoso/Minden Pictures, 21 Frans Lanting, 22 Cyril Ruoso/Minden Pictures, 24 Terry Whittaker
Nature Picture Library 7 Andy Rouse, 19 Suzi Eszterhas
Shutterstock back cover Eric Isselée